The Instructional Media Library

Volume Number 2

COMMUNITY RESOURCES

Rulon Kent Wood
Department of Instructional Media
Utah State University

James E. Duane
Series Editor

Educational Technology Publications
Englewood Cliffs, New Jersey 07632

Library of Congress Cataloging in Publication Data

Wood, Rulon Kent.
    Community resources.

    (The Instructional media library ; v. no. 2)
    Bibliography: p.
    1. Community and school. I. Title. II. Series:
Instructional media library ; v. no. 2.
LC215.W57   370.19'31   80-20963
ISBN 0-87778-162-1

Printed in the United States of America.

Library of Congress Catalog Card Number:
80-20963

International Standard Book Number:
0-87778-162-1

First Printing: January, 1981.

Table of Contents

COMMUNITY RESOURCES

1.

Introduction

Community resources are situations through which learners come into firsthand contact with people, places, and things in the community around them. In educational theory, such resources are any materials, agencies, activities, or persons in a community that may be utilized by a school program to provide learning experiences. The most common uses of such resources occur through the use of field trips and resource persons. Community resources have been further defined by one authority as:

> Anything in the community outside the schools that has educative value and is within the scope of school use. For example, museums, theaters, courts, libraries, industries, parks, playgrounds, etc., including outstanding individuals and other human resources.[1]

Some educators have assumed that emphasis upon use of community volunteer programs, community schools, and greater utilization of community resources is of recent origin. John Dewey, recognized as the most influential American philosopher of education, stressed the relationship between the community and education in *The School and Society:*

> From the standpoint of the child, the great waste in the school comes from his inability to utilize the experiences he gets outside the school in any complete and free way within the school itself; while on the other hand, he is unable to apply in daily life what he is learning in school. That is the isolation of the school—its isolation from life.[2]

Figure 1

Any city offers a great number of learning resources, whether it be Salt Lake City, Los Angeles, Philadelphia, or Cedar Rapids, Iowa. The local telephone directory may serve as one key index to learning resources in any community. (Photo courtesy Salt Lake Area Chamber of Commerce.)

The purpose of using the total community as an educational resource is to bring the school, the student, and real life into communication with one another. When this is done effectively, the result is that the school and the community of learners gain greater insight and appreciation of their community, and the community-at-large gains greater appreciation and understanding of the schools. These results increase the support of the community for the schools and help to keep the curriculum and learning experiences in the school a relevant part of the community.

Figure 2

Listings of Learning Resources. Three examples of listings of learning resources include *Industrial Opportunities*, depicting lists available from local Chamber of Commerce Offices; *Invitation to Learning*, which describes some of the community resources of a State University; and the *Yellow Pages of Learning Resources*. (Photo courtesy USU Center for Instructional Product Development, Logan, Utah.)

Applications of educational resources to community study may be beneficial to learners, teachers, and the community. One application involved a group of senior high school students working on the principle that statistics prove a need. The students conducted a traffic count outside their school to justify the provision of a crosswalk through a recently widened street, thereby providing more efficient flow to a shopping center. The students discovered that an average of 431 vehicles passed the area each hour. This information was then presented to the road department and police commission, thus demonstrating that statistics do prove a need.[3]

Figure 3

Young and old learners appreciate a trip to Living Historical Farms in Utah. Displays on Farming the Arid West lend special emphasis to the development of irrigation and farming in this country. Water systems from the past, old but "running" farm machinery, animals, and harvesting processes may be observed firsthand and may add special learning resources and appreciation to today's modern technology.

Some educators have provided novel and unique means of developing guides to community resources for learning. One of the most complete of the general guides is the *Yellow Pages of Learning Resources.*[4] This guide advocates the notion that learning is not confined to the classroom. The *Yellow Pages* is a catalog of 70 alphabetically arranged categories consisting of people (28 examples, ranging from bricklayer to union leader); places in the community (29 entries, from banks to the zoo) for supporting learning activities; and processes (13 examples, ranging from city planning to weather forecasting) which may be observed in communities to facilitate learning.

Use of community resources in support of learning in the schools is not new but has been reemphasized by recent developments. The developments of the open education concept, the community school, and career education have focused greater attention on the importance of community resources. More recently, the concept of "action-learning" has stressed the need for using community resources for educational purposes.[5]

The lack of a current text which gives guidelines in the effective use of community resources for education purposes has prompted the writing of this book. It is designed to give educators, including teachers, media specialists, librarians, and administrators, an overview and understanding of the processes and procedures which will enhance use of resource persons, services, agencies, and materials available in every community.

Notes

1. Carter V. Good, Ed. *Dictionary of Education.* Second Edition. New York: McGraw-Hill, 1959, p. 114.
2. As quoted in the special issue "Community Resources." *Man/Society/Technology,* December, 1975, p. 1.

3. Colin J. Marsh. "Whatever Happened to Local Community Studies?" *The Clearing House,* February, 1976, p. 260.
4. Richard Saul Wurman, Ed. *Yellow Pages of Learning Resources.* Cambridge: MIT Press, 1972.
5. "Action Education." Special Issue of the *National Association of Secondary School Principals Bulletin,* November, 1974.

2.

Objectives

General Objectives

Upon completion of the reading and study of this book, teachers, media specialists, librarians, administrators, and others will be able to survey, identify, describe, catalog, and effectively use community resources in support of the teaching-learning process.

Specific Objectives

- Survey local communities to identify resources available for learners in a particular instructional setting or class.
- List procedures for conducting community surveys.
- Explain, in writing, several effective techniques for planning and conducting field trips.
- Describe a program for effectively using community resource persons in school settings.
- Identify and name several institutions and agencies in communities which may be used as learning resources, such as museums, zoos, aquariums, planetariums, art galleries, banks, and industries; and demonstrate how they may be related to what is being taught in the schools.
- Describe procedures for identifying resource persons

in the larger communities of the state or the nation and explain their use as learning resources through Telelectures.

- Finally, using this book, a local telephone directory, and a number of blank cards, set up a resources file, including several sources for each of the following: field trips, resource persons, instructional materials, and institutions that may be used as resources in the classroom.

Because the community—local, state, or national—holds great potential for learning resources, it is intended that this book will encourage the creative and effective utilization of such assets.

The application of community resources to the needs of schools and learners is limited only by the imagination, planning, and follow-through of the educators responsible. In this time of curtailed budgets in all sectors of public life, community resources offer a tremendous wealth for learning that goes beyond budgetary limitations. The use of community resources curtails the isolation from life of which John Dewey spoke in his book, *The School and Society*, mentioned in the Introduction. The effective use of community resources to support education "links learning with life."

3.

The Community Resources Survey

The community resources survey is the first step to be taken by educators to utilize the local environment in the teaching-learning process. Among the values in making the survey and involving students are:

- Increased awareness and appreciation of the economic, social, political, and environmental institutions and agencies in the community.
- Deeper understanding and appreciation of the systematic approach to studying the community and problems through the developed skills of collecting, observing, classifying, and analyzing data.
- Further development of personality and communication skills through cooperative contacts with leaders and workers involved in community activities.
- Increased understanding of the processes of society and the community through the interpretation of activities that affect students/learners and their families.
- Greater appreciation for the origin, history, and development of community value patterns.

Community resources surveys have been found to be useful in helping learners to understand better the basic life processes, the problems, and the issues of common concern in the community. Such processes help students learn more directly how citizens:

(1) utilize their natural environment;

(2) make a living in the community;

(3) share the burdens and benefits of citizenship;

(4) exchange ideas and effect changes;

(5) maintain health and safety within the community;

(6) meet their religious and social needs;

(7) improve family life;

(8) accept newcomers into the community; and

(9) secure their education and training.

The traditional involvement pattern for schools has been expressed by one writer[1] concerned with the process of linking the teacher and the school to the parents and the community, diagrammatically, as shown in Figure 4.

Obviously, this degree of involvement is not enough. Parents/community members have indicated a continuing concern about the lack of understanding of school programs and have shown a desire to be more aware of these programs. They would normally welcome the chance to become part of the school process. Teacher/school and parents/community groups must work together in a planned, meaningful way to identify, organize, implement, and evaluate the use of community resources in the teaching-learning process. The proposed involvement would be diagrammatically expressed as shown in Figure 5.

The proposed involvement would demand continuous evaluation of the school program. As part of the evaluation process of using community resources, debriefing sessions should incorporate feedback from all concerned groups. A Community Resource Council may be developed to make the evaluation process routine and continuous.

The community-wide survey is one of the essentials to effective utilization of community resources. A single person will be ineffective in conducting a full-scale community resources survey, but such a survey usually *begins* with one person. A small survey in conjunction with a single class may

Figure 4

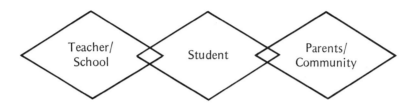

Traditional involvement of the teacher and the school through the student with the parents and the community.

Figure 5

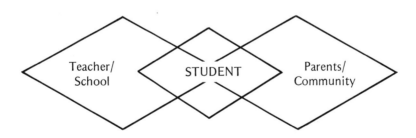

The proposed involvement of the teacher and the school with the student, the parents, and the community in the learning process.

demonstrate to others the effectiveness of using community resources to support learning. However, more effective surveys will result if plans are made to facilitate the continuous survey and evaluation, rather than "let's do it and get it over with."

Communities change, people and agencies come and go, and the community resources survey must be considered as a continuous process if it is to be effective. The "one-time" survey will be helpful, but it will soon become obsolete. The community resources survey is a continuous process used to add and to delete assets which may be used to enhance learning.

Team Efforts in Constructing the Survey

In a recently completed national needs assessment which identified the skills and knowledge necessary for teachers to effectively use learning resources through the school library media center programs, the item placed at highest priority by the national panel of experts was that teachers "be able to work as part of an instructional team in achieving instructional goals and objectives."[2]

Team efforts for constructing the community resources survey involve teachers, media specialists, administrators, students, and community members in the task of providing more effective means for achieving instructional goals and objectives.

Many teachers and administrators would use community resources if they had access to information about the resources as well as experience in using the resources recorded to assist them in their instructional planning. In addition, they require means to use such resources. For years, teachers have made sporadic use of community resources, usually by field trips. In the past, these trips have been to predominant industrial or special community points of interest. The students have been "curious," as if they were on

Figure 6

Teachers should be able to survey local communities to identify resources which would enhance the learning of their students. Above, a teacher is consulting with a manager/owner of a local audio-visual firm to arrange for art, business, and photography students to visit the shop. Such visits may promote career education goals of the school as well as subject areas. (Photo courtesy Salt Lake Area Chamber of Commerce.)

miniature sight-seeing trips, rather than viewing the experience as related directly to classroom studies.

The community-wide survey is one of the keys to effective use of resources for learning, rather than having a "sight-seeing tour." The effects of the survey are widespread. Information is gathered, and many persons are involved in the process. The persons taking the survey, the resource persons of the community, the public in general, but especially parents become more interested in what the schools are doing. *Involvement* is the element which pulls the entire community together in the educational process. The community survey has the potential to achieve that involvement. It may serve the purpose of creating more involvement by using parent volunteers in the survey along with school personnel. Community involvement in the schools has been too often an accidental occurrence.

A Systematic Approach to the Survey

The community resources survey should be planned with care and should answer the following questions: Why are we taking the survey? What do we hope to discover? What do we want to tell people in the process? What results do we want from the community resources survey? When the survey is completed, who will write and organize the results into a usable resources file? How will the file be kept up-to-date? What evaluation will be present in the survey to keep it up-to-date?

Conducting the Community Survey

Extensive information about community services, places of interest, agencies, and resource people is necessary in order to use the community as a learning laboratory. Teachers may frequently live outside the communities in which they teach and have limited knowledge of the community in which their students live. The media center may have extensive information on film and books of places and people in distant locations, but the materials may be inadequate with regard to information of local surroundings. Every community is rich in resources, which may be used to enhance the teaching-learning process.

It has been found that prior to making community surveys, teachers questioned had very little knowledge of community resources. Many did not use community resources; many believed field trips were not allowed, although the district had readily made buses available for any field trip that would enhance a unit of study. When teachers are made aware of community resources, most are eager to use them.

Figure 7

These blast furnaces depict unique learning resources which are available in industrial settings; they are important to consider with the community resources survey. They provide a learning resource which is difficult to duplicate through audio-visual means. (Photo courtesy Utah Travel Council.)

In conducting community surveys, permission should be obtained from the administration of the district. The Committee on Human Resources of the Metropolitan School Study Council carried out a survey of the New York City area to initiate a planned program. This group suggested that three important elements should be present for the successful survey:[3]

- Spark and enthusiasm must come from the schools.
- Personal contact is essential; reception at school must be cordial and friendly.
- Provisions must be made for evaluation and revision of the resources file.

The following information is suggested to be collected for the resources file:

- Time the resource is available.
- Subject area where it may be used.
- Size of group wishing to use the resource.
- Grade levels for which the resource is suitable.
- Safety precautions which may be necessary.
- The supervision required.
- How to contact and schedule the resource for use.
- Amount of time necessary for a trip to the resource, and the time which may be profitably spent with the resource.

Summary

As teachers, specialists, and administrators seek to achieve some of their most important objectives, they will do well to identify and explore community learning resources and include them in their planning. Consider the relationship of community resources to these educational goals:

- Understanding social life.
- Developing citizenship and civic responsibility.
- Achieving vocational understanding and economic efficiency.
- Self-realization of the individual.

Clearly, the use of community resources in support of these learning goals may give stronger support to the achievement of the specific objectives of education.

Using community resources provides extraordinary opportunities for teachers to introduce tangible sorts of learning experiences to achieve many of the important goals of education. In essence, the community can be a laboratory for learners to collect and study data, make decisions, and test their decisions with other data. The "concreteness" and the "real-worldliness" are likely to stimulate a much higher degree of personal interest and commitment to learning.

Notes

1. JoAnne Buggey. "Citizenship and Community Involvement," *Social Studies and the Elementary Teacher,* March, 1976, p. 161.
2. Rulon Kent Wood. *Using Media Centers in Education: The NATUL Project.* Logan, Utah: Instructional Media Department of Utah State University, 1976.
3. Committee on Human Resources of the Metropolitan School Study Council. *Fifty Teachers to a Classroom.* New York: Macmillan Co., 1953, pp. 1-8.

4.

The Community Resources File

In the Introduction, community resources were defined as anything in the community outside the schools that has instructional value and is within the scope of school use. The resources provide situations through which learners come into firsthand contact with people, places, and things in their community. These resources include organizations, institutions, neighborhoods, or areas of the community. Such resources include community leaders and officials. Use of these resources may involve listening, observing, and interviewing, as well as recording data collected in the process. The examination of tools, machines, and reports, or doing activities provide real-life opportunities to learn by participating in community life. These situations as well as social and political services are all part of community life.

The ideal situation would be to have the central school district, through the district media center, maintain a community resources survey which could be reflected in a catalog in the form of looseleaf binders. The first edition of the survey inventory would be issued as a looseleaf catalog, updated with the printing and distribution of sheets which would be added as new community resources are identified and described for use. Whenever a community resource is to be discontinued or no longer used as such, an instruction sheet could be issued to update the community resources catalog. In this way, the catalog could be kept as a continuing inventory of community resources to be used for educational purposes.

Before such resources may be effectively utilized in the teaching-learning process, they must be systematically surveyed and described in the resources file. It is fitting that many recent texts dealing with library/media centers emphasize the importance of the resources file. In addition to maintaining an index to the library media center's collection, the media specialist should also take professional responsibility for organizing and publicizing the availability of the file of local community resources and contacts. It is suggested that deletions and additions be made as the need arises, with the file being developed as a joint concern of faculty and library media staff. It is further suggested that each time a field trip or a visit is made, or a speaker from the community has come to the school as a resource person, or an industrial site is visited, an evaluation sheet indicating the educational value and merit of the experience be placed in the community resources file. It may grow to be a multi-volume file.

During the planning of instructional support with classroom teachers, media specialists frequently have opportunities to suggest significant community resources. In order to make this service functional, data must be gathered in order to describe and inform teachers about the resources, and vice versa. Some forms have proved helpful for data collection on agencies, businesses, resource persons, and sites which have instructional potential and uses. Specific items could include the name of the agency or persons, addresses, major products or services, a brief description of the resources, the subject area of the curriculum to which the resources apply, and the grade level most applicable. Other information may be the number of students who may visit or use the resource, the times available, the contact persons for making arrangements,

Figure 8

This refurbished mansion was once occupied by Brigham Young. Known as the Beehive House, it provides a special learning resource in Salt Lake City, as these students will soon find out. Every community has many special historical sites and homes which should be included on resources surveys. (Photo courtesy Salt Lake Valley Convention and Visitors Bureau.)

Figure 9

This Dinosaur Quarry provides a unique learning resource. It is an unusual resource, but many communities have resources which might serve to enhance learning in the life sciences. Such resources should be included in the community resources file to encourage teachers and students to utilize them in their teaching and learning. (Photo courtesy Utah Travel Council.)

Figure 10

This coal-powered electrical generating plant provides a good site for students to learn about energy and air pollution problems. With the importance of coal growing daily as the supply of oil decreases, students should have great interest in such resources so as to make learning more relevant to the world around them. (Photo courtesy of Utah Travel Council.)

how far in advance the arrangements need to be made, and the costs (if any) for using the resource.

Sample Forms

Examples of forms are given on the following pages, taken from sources discussing the use of community resources. They could be modified for local purposes to better serve individual needs as necessary. Design of such forms is an important part of setting up the resources file. See Figures 11, 12, and 13.

Figure 11

Sample Community Resources Form

1. Name of agency, business, site, or resource person ....
    ....

2. Address ....
    .... Phone Number ....

3. Name of contact person ....

4. Major products, services, or experiences to be given or observed ....
    ....

5. Is the number of students who may visit limited? If so, please note
    maximum and minimum numbers.
    Maximum .... Minimum ....

6. Is the age limit of students a factor to be considered? ....
    What is the suggested minimum age of student visitors? ....

7. Are specific times set aside for visitors or use?
    Time .... Day(s) ....

8. Should visitors be requested to bring any specific items with them?
    ....

9. Is the type of wearing apparel of the visitors important? If so, please
    describe ....

10. How far in advance should the visit be arranged? ....
    .... Suggested ....

11. If there is a charge for usage or visiting, please note below.
    ....

12. Curriculum subject areas to which the resource may apply.
    ....

Form modified from Nancy Polette, *Developing Methods of Inquiry: A Source Book for Elementary Media Personnel.* Metuchen, N.J.: Scarecrow Press, 1973, p. 140.

Figure 12

Sample Community Resources Form

---

1.   Name ....

2.   Location ....

3.   Telephone ....

4.   Contact ....

5.   Hours ....

6.   Fee ....

7.   When to schedule ....

8.   Suggested transportation ....

9.   Type of program or learning experience ....
     ....

10. Grade level suitability ....

11. Curriculum tie-in ....

12. Evaluations ....
     ....

13. Special preparation or comments ....
     ....

Modified from Ruth Ann Davies, *The School Library Media Center: A Force for Educational Excellence.* Second Edition. New York: R.R. Bowker, 1974, p. 89.

Figure 13

Sample Community Resources Form

Dear Patron:

Would you be willing to share your occupation, hobby, talents, experience, or travels with the boys and girls of .... School? If you are able to give us a little of your time, we feel sure that the experience would be a real learning opportunity for the students. We would be most grateful if you would complete the items below and return this questionnaire to the school.

Thank you,

.... Principal

Name ....
        Address ....
        Phone ....

Please note the area which you would be willing to share:

Occupation ....

Hobby ....

Travel ....

Other ....
        ....

For what age level would your talk, demonstration, or materials be most suitable?
....

When might you be available to visit the school?

Day(s) .... Time(s) ....

How far in advance do you wish to be contacted?
....

Setting Up a Community Resources File

When the forms have been completed by door-to-door survey, by telephone survey, or by student survey, a community resources file may be established in the media center or may be published by the school or the district.

An entry which might be made in the 8½ x 11 inch looseleaf binder may be more extensive and could include the following:

Name: Hansen Planetarium

Location: 15 South State Street
             Salt Lake City, Utah

Telephone: 364-3611

Contact: Any of the reservationists

Hours: Monday—Friday (9-5:30 and 7-10:30)
          Saturday (9-5:30 and 7-11:30)

Fee: Group rates are . . . .

    Special rates for ten or more people—information obtained
    through reservationist

When to schedule: Two or more days in advance

Transportation: Salt Lake busline (Utah Transit Authority) makes
                 stop at planetarium

Type of program or learning experiences provided: "Legacies" dealing with Ameri-
                 can achievement in space

Grade level suitability: Should be interesting to those age five and
                          above

Curriculum tie-in: Solar system

Evaluation:

Although 8½ x 11 inch looseleaf binders are recommended, some authorities prefer 3 x 5 inch card files. These cards may be added to the card catalog or placed in a separate file. In either format, a person should be designated and assigned to maintain the file and to keep the survey in process.

Entries in the file should be made under the company, person, or site name, and an added entry should be made under subject. When cards are used, the reverse side may provide space for noting visits and evaluations along with other notations. If the information concerning the resource is extensive, multiple cards may be used. An example of a card entry follows:

```
Smith's Fine Meats, Inc.
30 West 700 N. St.
792-1234

Hours:  9-5 M–F       Ages: 12 and up
Contact:    Mr. D. Smith, 792-1234
            Two weeks before
            Groups limited to 15
            Wear low-heeled shoes

NO CHARGE
MEAT PROCESSING: Grinding, Curing, and Smoking
```

Summary

There are many resources in any community which may provide useful experiences in the teaching-learning process. Local speakers, government officials, such as mayors and council persons, performers, college professors, open-pit mines, public parks and zoos, lumber and cabinet shops, museums, airports, and many other resources may prove worthwhile to list in the file.

Speakers and performers listed in the file will be able to

Figure 14

Inside the Hansen Planetarium. This planetarium provides an excellent community resource to be utilized by teachers. The facility provides a variety of prepared presentations (shows) on space travel, astronomy, and other topics related to space science.

Figure 15

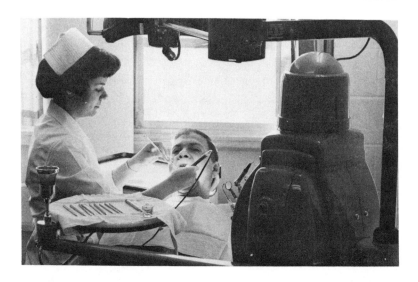

Arrangements made with professional persons, such as dentists, physicians, attorneys, social workers, psychologists, and others, may be an extremely important resource for career education as well as for other areas of the curriculum. Most will allow planned visits, or individual students to "work out of a vest-pocket" arrangement on a short-term basis to learn what various professionals do and what the professions mean in community life and services. (Photo courtesy Broome Technical Community College, Binghamton, New York.)

hold the attention of audiences as well as have items of educational value to convey. The local artists may even agree to serve as "artists in residence" at local schools. Organizations such as the YMCA, the YWCA, the Boy Scouts, the Girl Scouts, or the Chamber of Commerce may be able to suggest other resources, or may have already compiled lists of their own which may save you much time in starting a community resources file. The nearby university may maintain lists of foreign visitors and students who may serve as resource persons. Teachers in the school district may have traveled extensively and may already have files or slides and artifacts to share with students. Many parents have collections of educational value, such as a father who raises prize sheep, an engineering consultant who has films of foreign countries, or an older sister who has developed a prize-winning science fair project. The local baker, auto-shop foreman, dentist, or business person may provide other sources for learning from the community. The local telephone office may have films and other materials of special worth to be used as learning resources which are unavailable elsewhere. Every community, rural or urban, has many potentially outstanding resources available, and school systems can profit significantly by developing and maintaining community resources files.

5.

Community Resources for
Group and Individualized Instruction

As group-oriented instruction gives way to more individualized instruction patterns and techniques, this new approach acquires many forms and is given numerous labels. In a recent computerized search of the ERIC system for reports and projects treating individualized learning, it was found that some 59 descriptors, all variants of the basic term "individualized instruction," were utilized.

With individualized instruction, new roles must be identified and defined for students and teachers. The student/learner becomes an investigator. Such learners are encouraged to think as scientists when they study science, practice behaviors exhibited by scientists, and become more involved in "real-life" learning experiences.

When students/learners deal with the subjects of history or social sciences, they are asked to take on the "eyes, views, and attitudes" common to historians and social scientists. The student is no longer simply exposed to information but is more responsible for self-learning as opposed to being "taught."

Teachers become coordinators of learning, members of teams, and planners and evaluators of learning. Principals become managers of behavioral-conceptual curricula and learning; creators of "selective discontent" with present programs, which may be improved. "Back to Basics" is back to real-life situations of the community by utilizing the basic resources available to learners and educators.

Content of learning is changing from textbook orientation with verbally delivered messages to other media which provide for inquiry into the environment, careers, and the "real" world of work. "Real-life" learning experiences in the community are perhaps most relevant to the effective use of community resources in education. The self-contained classrooms and graded and group-paced instruction are giving way to individualized instruction and greater use of community resources.

Because of traditional educational preoccupation with group instruction, little has been suggested for individuals to use community resources. Community resources study has been limited primarily to sites for field trips, such as museums, businesses, and landmark areas. These same resources may be used for individual study, if such settings are developed as part of learning packages in order to provide design and purpose for individual learners.

One of the best examples of using community resources in education is a small, rural school in Lindon, Utah. The Lindon School provided a unique setting for developing community resources to enhance and enrich learning experiences. Lindon School was planned to test new ideas which might be useful at elementary schools elsewhere. The thrust of the planning centered on environmental education, defined as the effective use of the natural environment to teach those parts of the curriculum that can be taught outdoors and to vitalize other parts through firsthand experiences.

The experiences provided by the Lindon School related to the curriculum areas of weather, trees, social studies, arithmetic, geology, health, and language arts, to name a few. The central idea behind the Lindon School was for students to explore and discover—to learn through observation—their own environment. Social and civic values were changed appreciably for the good from the Lindon program. Group cooperation and individual learning increased, with personal, school, and civic pride developing more effectively because of the efficient utilization of community resources.

Higher education is also beginning to review the need for more effective use of community resources in education. University administrators, faculty, and researchers are concerned with the relationship of the colleges and universities to the community, reflected in such recent conference reports as *University and Community: The New Partnership* and *The University and Community Services.*[1] Provocative topics of concern reported at these conferences were directed to "the neighborhood and its institutions; poverty; consumer fraud; economic growth; the city and the museum; health; the city and the novel; education and model cities; the university and the professions; and the anatomy of change." These reflect new concerns of universities and colleges for the community, and vice versa.

The concern for individualizing learning in higher education is also reflected by the dramatic shift in thinking from overcrowded lecture halls to something much more humanized, such as using community resources for individual study through internships and independent study. Society seems to be advocating "education for each" rather than "education for all" in the old sense of democratized education.[2]

The Community Resources Grid

One way of initiating better use of community resources is to develop a community resources grid. It brings into perspective and planning the various community resources which may have potential use in group or individualized instruction. A resources grid may list horizontally across the top the various ways of using the resources, which are listed vertically along the left side. The grid becomes a vital part of teacher planning for use of community resources, because it may allow the identification of resources which are neglected and seldom used along with those which may tend to be overused and overloaded. The grid becomes another tool with which to plan strategies for individual, independent, and group learning with community resources.

The programs and services of the various community agencies, such as zoos, aquariums, museums, industries and businesses, governmental agencies, libraries, and transportation agencies, are among those which might be considered for inclusion in the resources grid. The idea of the resources grid is to provide a map of services available from the organizations, agencies, governmental groups, or individuals in the community whose services may contribute in meaningful ways to the learning of students. The grid may be a rather comprehensive map, or it may be directed to some specific instructional problem. For example, a goal of "to improve the reading scores of all sixth grade students at 'X' middle school who read one or more years below grade level" could be directed to utilizing local doctors, optical associations, the Rotary and Lions Clubs, a university reading clinic, and the PTA.

The community resources grid may be used as a general approach or may be detailed and specific. For example, emphasis might be placed upon individual uses, such as internship arrangements or independent study. Museums, libraries, businesses, and various governmental agencies have attempted to make such arrangements more accessible in recent years. The resources grid provides for the initial planning map of community resources after the survey and the community resources file have been developed. It becomes a shortened index to community resources and may be developed by individual teachers or groups of teachers and other specialists.

Notes

1. Albert Fein and Elliot Gatner, Eds. *University and Community: The New Partnership.* Brooklyn, New York: Long Island University, 1971. F. Robert Paulsen, Ed. *The University and Community Services: A Conference Sponsored by the Community Resources Project.* Tucson, Arizona: University of Arizona, 1969.
2. Dyckman W. Vermilye, Ed. *Individualizing the System: Current Issues in Higher Education.* San Francisco, Jossey-Bass, 1976.

6.

Procedural Guidelines for Use of Community Resources

Community resources for use in education include people, places, things, and activities used with learners. Often these resources are considered prime sources for teaching students to become good citizens. They may deal with governmental agencies, businesses and industrial settings, natural resources, human resources, and geographical or special topographic features and sites. The effective utilization of these resources may have a salutary effect on students, teachers, parents, and other citizens who participate. Instructional programs which include use of community resources are greatly enriched in the process, and learning becomes more relevant and meaningful to students/learners. When such resources are effectively utilized in the teaching-learning processes of the schools, there is an excellent opportunity for enhancing communication between schools and the community.

Those using community resources effectively should plan and establish guidelines for such utilization. This chapter outlines some considerations and suggested guidelines.

Classifying Community Resources
Specialists are persons such as professionals, artists, and industrial, business, and service workers. Bankers, farmers, merchants, homemakers, and hobbyists are among the many ex-

amples of individuals who may be utilized in education through talks, illustrated lectures, demonstrations, and interviews regarding their respective fields. In other situations, individual students or small groups may seek information from these specialists at their homes or places of work. Specialists may serve as learning resources both at and away from the classroom. They may be used on a one-to-one specialist-student relationship or as a human resource for groups of students. Specialists are among the most accessible and the most used of all community learning resources.

Parents of students are among the most valuable human resources. They may either support the school program or be antagonistic toward its activities, depending upon their understanding of the goals, objectives, and procedures of teachers, counselors, and media specialists. Parents are often taken for granted, and their assistance provides an excellent opportunity for communicating with them. Those who have already shown interest in the schools as members of the PTA or other school-related activities are the most likely to respond positively and will welcome the opportunity to serve the school.

Agency representatives are persons who are affiliated with civic, social, service, or cultural agencies, including officers and committee chairpersons. Service clubs, unions, libraries, art, music, and historical societies, along with professional organizations, usually have education-related committees and provide other community resources for use in educational settings. They often provide services to the schools. Several agencies provide career days and opportunities for students to meet successful leaders in the various professional and occupational areas. Although these groups may wish to inform the students about their respective goals and functions, the "advertising efforts" are usually minimal and those representing such agencies provide important, valuable community resources to the schools.

Figure 16

Libraries provide many book and audio-visual learning resources which may be unavailable in the schools. Public libraries are changing with the times by providing media production facilities, recording studios, lecture halls, and special educational programs for the community. Such resources should not be taken for granted; they should be analyzed and cataloged for the community resources file. (Photo courtesy Cazenovia College, New York.)

Business and industrial representatives are persons who are involved in manufacturing, agriculture, banking and financial activities, transportation, mining, retail and wholesale businesses, construction trades, etc. These groups often provide lectures, demonstrations, and "on-site" visits for students. They are normally willing to participate in vocational and distributive education and work/study programs, where students may learn from firsthand experiences about the businesses and industries. They also provide teachers the opportunity to improve their skills and knowledge of such establishments.

Figure 17

The petroleum industry is becoming very important. Some communities have such learning resources as this oil well on their own "door steps." Students learn to appreciate natural resources more when given opportunities to learn on a first-hand basis. (Photo courtesy Orange Coast College.)

Government representatives provide a rich reservoir of talent. Observation of "on-the-job" activities of people in government agencies is valuable. A Telelecture from Washington, D.C., with a Senator, Representative, or government official may add great insights. Visits to state capitals, city and county buildings, courts, and legislatures add dimensions to learning which may not be duplicated by other means.

Citizens' advisory boards and committees have been successfully utilized as community resources for many schools by providing coordination and suggestions. The committee is normally representative of a cross-section of persons in the community. Appointments are made by the appropriate administrator, with the board of education approving such appointments. It is important for the advisory body to have a means to define and establish its respective duties and responsibilities, such as by a constitution and by-laws. Members should be appointed for a specific term, with terms staggered to insure that experienced members are serving at all times. The chairperson of the advisory board or committee should always be a lay person rather than an educator, with a secretary being a school-related person to take minutes, send notices of meetings and programs, and perform other duties to insure the success of the advisory group.

Widely traveled citizens and those who have lived for extended periods of time in other areas of this country and foreign countries are valuable learning resources, which add understanding of conditions in other countries and other parts of the state and nation. Within limitations, these persons are normally willing to give of their time and talents.

The following are suggested guidelines in insuring good relationships and productive use of community resources:

1. Be direct but complete in explaining the need for the resource aid.
2. Use good judgment with regard to the amount of aid requested.
3. Make the request in person if possible, and then follow-up with a letter confirming the details discussed during the personal interview.
4. Thoroughly inform the resource person or agency of the requirements of the visit.
5. Offer friendly, constructive suggestions to improve performance if the resource aid is a continuing one.
6. Show friendliness and courtesy to the resource person performing an assigned task or associated with the community resource utilization.

Resource persons who are to appear before teachers for in-service work, or before students, must be oriented to their assignments. A definite understanding of time limits must be established as well as procedures for question-and-answer periods. Details for required projectors and equipment, along with other paraphernalia needed by the resource persons should be made well in advance of their use. Pre- and postpresentation reviews with the resource person and with learners are advised if maximum success and productivity are desired. Finally, teachers and students should write personal letters of appreciation to maintain good relations with those persons who are providing community resources. Preplanning and follow-up help to provide good learning experiences for students and cement school and community relations in a positive fashion.

Guidelines for conducting field and study trips are of utmost importance. When such trips require no vehicular transportation, the following steps are suggested:

1. Orient students thoroughly to the objectives of the visit.
2. Make all necessary prearrangements for observing the resource.
3. Be as specific as possible in outlining safety precautions (such as visits to construction sites).
4. Continue to focus the students' attention on the trip's objectives as the students observe various resources.
5. Assign a leader whose duties are to keep the students grouped together so that explanations can be heard by everyone (usually these leaders are students).
6. Discuss, review, and evaluate the trip and its objectives after returning to the classroom.

For study trips and tours requiring transportation, additional guidelines should be considered. The study trip is only one step in the students' learning in the community and should be provided to achieve specific objectives developed by teachers and students. When transportation is needed, these guidelines should be followed:

1. Make the necessary transportation arrangements needed for the trip.
2. Outline each student's personal and financial responsibilities.
3. Have a written memorandum of understanding signed by the parents, student, administrator, counselor, or teacher concerned; the memorandum might indicate parental approval of the trip or tour and acceptance of financial responsibilities, penalties for student misconduct, and legal and other responsibilities of the parents, the student, and the professional school person.

Community Study Liability

On community study trips, it is suggested that one adult leader be provided to supervise no more than 25 students, and on extended trips and tours, the ratio should be increased to one adult to supervise no more than 15 students. The ratio may be varied as circumstances dictate, but this has proved to be a realistic supervision formula to follow.

In these activities, the matter of teacher liability is one to be thoroughly understood. In most states, the liability of teachers or other representatives of school boards is recognized only in instances in which actual negligence can be proved. Authorized, properly supervised study trips are generally regarded as being no different, as far as liability is concerned, from other schoolground or classroom activities. Some state codes contain special restrictions, and these should be checked by teachers. School administrators will normally have access to official policy statements on the subject of liability.

1. The school board should acknowledge community study as a desirable enrichment experience and an integral part of the school's regular program.

2. The principal should make the school board's policy known to teachers.

3. The school board should provide liability insurance for the teaching staff. In Utah, Wisconsin, and other states, school boards are legally authorized to expend public money for this purpose.

4. The teacher and principal should plan community-resource activities which will help accomplish the goals and the objectives of existing curriculum plans. Such activities should not be confused with festivals, holiday excursions, and other out-of-school activities of dubious educational value.

5. The teacher, with the guidance of the principal, should arrange transportation via school bus or other bonded carriers, which are required by law to carry liability insurance.

6. Teachers should never assume responsibility for conducting pupils through a plant or industry, but should arrange to have the management supply a guide. As soon as the tour is ended, the teacher should have the pupils return to the school immediately, again by a properly insured carrier.

7. The use of a parental permission letter informs parents that community-resource experiences take place out of the classroom and are an acknowledged part of the school program. This allows parents to restrict their children from this kind of activity, if they wish. But the granting of parental permission does not absolve the teacher who takes the class into the community from exercising the same reasonable care he or she is expected to exercise in the classroom.

The teacher should be expected to take the initiative and leadership to plan and evaluate community resources, such as study trips and the use of resource persons. The teacher must be the individual who decides when a community-resource experience has value in the teaching-learning process. The teacher deals with the preliminary preparation, discussion of study objectives, actual use of the resources, the follow-up discussion, review, and evaluation, and the developing projects and learning that grow out of the use of community resources.

Community Resources and Study Trip Information

The following form is suggested in planning for the use of community resources, with information obtained from the community resources file as discussed in Chapter 4. Additional information obtained during future use may be helpful to update the community resources file.*

Place of Resource .... Address .... Phone ....

Person who should be reached in advance of trip/use ....

Age level of learners who would benefit from such study ....

Number of learners who could be taken through or use the resource at one time ....(maximum-minimum)..................................

Is guide service/information service provided? ....

Are groups divided into smaller groups? ....

If so, how many learners would be in each group? ....

Days of the week on which visitors would be most welcome ....
....

Hours at which visitors could be received most conveniently ....
....

Time required to make the trip or use resource ....

Parking accommodations ....

*Form suggested by Professor Brenda Branyan of Utah State University, Department of Instructional Media.

Special requirements of the plant/business/resource ....
....

Material that can be learned from the plant/business/resource ....
....

Films, pamphlets, or exhibit materials that can be provided to help groups understand better the plant, business, or resource (please list any that are available and describe them briefly) ....
....
....

7.

Case Studies

Students have a need to be educated and trained in the realities of the world beyond formal classrooms and school settings. A general criticism prevails that few teachers make available to students the opportunities the community offers in the way of learning resources. As educators work to achieve some of their most significant objectives, they should review case studies in which community resources have been used with a variety of students.

The purpose of this chapter is to touch upon selected case studies which may lead teachers to create their own strategies for using the community as an open classroom full of meaningful learning experiences. The traditional classroom and its false boundaries for learning are in need of redefinition to an open experience in which educators and learners become responsive to the opportunities in the total environment. Whether the learner is in a rural or urban setting, the community provides unlimited opportunities to enhance learning. The case studies are presented as indicative of what creative educators may do to break down the isolation of the school from the community.

Mathias Township High School
Mathias Township is located in southern Alger County and

is between the cities of Marquette and Escanaba in Michigan's Upper Peninsula. It includes a number of small rural farming communities interspersed among state and federally owned forest lands. The population of the entire community at the turn of this decade was fewer than 750 people.

The major goal of the program developed at Mathias was to provide students the opportunity to relate to people beyond their own personal realms in a positive way. Subgoals of this program include:

(1) to gain a real understanding of the value of money with regard to total cost of living;

(2) to discover various career and vocational possibilities; and

(3) to gain proficiency at achieving pluralistic objectives in the confines of a small-group setting.

The program was designed as a six-week experience integrated into the American Government course curriculum. The approach was to associate "current events" with American Government, as reflected in a task sheet developed to involve students in activities.

Classroom speakers from the community presented many facets of life. A young couple from the community discussed with the class members their changing relationships through five years of married life, such as moving away from home for the first time, the problems associated with getting a job, responsibilities faced in rearing children, and how their first child changed their earlier life style. Another person brought to the class from the community was a counseling psychologist who explored with the class the concept of "self-identity" and other factors of individual development. Two young widows recounted their personal experiences related to the deaths of their husbands. Field trips were taken to a Strategic Air Command Base and to the cities of Milwaukee and Chicago. Museums, theaters, large schools, and an art institute were among the community resources utilized on those field trips.

Evaluations were both positive and negative, as one would expect. However, the students involved repeatedly expressed that they felt they had established positive experimental relationships with people outside their home communities and schools. For the students involved in the Mathias High School program, the real world became their classroom and the use of community resources provided enrichment to their learning.

Logan School District

Logan is a university town of some 25,000 residents and is the home of Utah State University.

The Logan City Volunteer program was begun in 1974 and continues to grow. It originated from a state PTA effort to encourage greater cooperation between schools and communities. The annual report of the program for 1978-79 showed a total of 122,524 hours devoted to the program. Volunteers range from university students serving as tutors to parents and community resource persons giving time to present special music, art, and other programs that teachers may request.

The goals of the Logan program are:

    (1) to help make more effective the process of public education;

    (2) to assist the professional staff in their responsibilities by offering needed services to children, as individuals or in small groups, which would supplement the work of classroom teachers;

    (3) to enrich the experiences of children beyond what is available in school;

    (4) to help develop resource materials for use in classrooms; and

    (5) to build a better understanding of schools and their programs among citizens, and to stimulate widespread support for public education.

The arts segment of the program has involved parents. Mothers and fathers take reproductions of paintings into classrooms each month and discuss them for 15 to 30 minutes. They tell about the artist, the period, techniques, style, use of color, and history, at the children's level. Activities are associated with the parent presentations to help the children identify and remember each painting and experience. These include creative writing, drawing pictures using similar colors and techniques, or arranging a group of objects for a still-life painting.

Salt Lake City Adopt-a-School Program

Business employees are paid for up to three hours of time given each week to the schools to enrich the curriculum and the learning experiences of students. The idea is to provide the community resources of various businesses to the school district. The program has grown to a point that in 1978-79 some 210,000 hours were given to the schools from 5,000 volunteers in the district-wide program.

Activities of the program, known as School Volunteers, Inc., are directed by a board of 28 persons representative of the community. All donate their time, with board members participating in the training of coordinators, volunteers, and professional staff; in evaluating each school's program throughout the year; in encouraging more community involvement; in preparing special materials; and in funding projects which are beyond the budget of the school district. A full-time executive director is hired to run this program in a community of about 175,000, serving a school population of some 24,500 students.

By adopting a school, the business or community organization tries to provide volunteers to fill the various needs of a particular school. Several Salt Lake City businesses are now releasing employees each week so they may serve as volunteers.

Philadelphia's Parkway Program

Begun more than a decade ago, the Parkway program remains viable as a major community resource program in the city of Philadelphia. Students may be found in city offices, museums, science centers, hospitals, theaters, and department stores. Courses in law enforcement may be taken with the police department; biology at the Academy of Natural Sciences; or library science at the public library.

The program continues to grow and contribute to the concept of using community resources to make learning and education more viable and meaningful.

The Dallas Theater Center

Housed in a handsome Frank Lloyd Wright designed edifice, this community resource is provided to students from ages four to 18 in Dallas, Texas. The Center offers a program to assist learners in acquiring self-expressive experiences not available normally in the schools. Sessions are held during the summer, after school, and on Saturdays. It is designed to be an exploration of art for all students.

Minneapolis Public Schools

Begun in 1970 under Title III (ESEA), the Guthrie Theater and the Walker Art Center are part of a plan to use the Twin City community resources. The school district initiated a successful community resources volunteer program, with courses in the visual and performing arts given daily outside the confines of the schools. Classes are open to all junior high and senior high school students, who are provided opportunities to learn from artists.

The Lyceum of the Monterey Peninsula

A unique non-profit organization named after the type of school established by Aristotle, the Lyceum provides another case study of effective use of community resources. It is supported by philanthropic-minded individuals and groups for the purpose of bringing students together in special seminars, conferences, and workshops dealing with a variety of topics. Serving the needs of students from kindergarten through the twelfth grade, the major purpose of the Lyceum as a community resource program is to "supplement and extend but not duplicate school offerings." Examples of programs include such topics as lifesaving conducted at the Coast Guard Station, introduction to medicine at the U.S. Army Health Clinic, animal care at the local animal hospital, introduction to aviation at the local airport, cartooning at a local public library, and horse care at a riding center.

The Executive High School Internships of America

Headquartered in New York City, another program of note assists school districts throughout the country to develop and implement special programs for junior and senior high school students.

Selection criteria include initiative, perseverance, creativity, leadership, sensitivity, and maturity. Students participate in a one-term leave-of-absence from all classes to work with key executives in their communities in such settings as government, business, media, arts, law, social services, health, and civic affairs. The students selected receive no salary, but their work sometimes leads to summer jobs and permanent employment.

The cases listed in this chapter were drawn from personal experiences, interviews, and the literature, such as B.A. Montiegel, "Total Life Simulation in the Rural School: A Successful Working Model," *Education*, Fall, 1978; L. Arbetman, L. Riekes, and S. Spiegel, "From Classroom to Courtroom: Using Legal Resource Persons," *Social Studies*, May-June, 1979; L. Adams, "Going Public: Community Based Student Writing," *Media and Methods*, February, 1979; M.B. Wine, "Classroom and Community: Partnership for Learning," *Business Education Forum*, February, 1979; *Extend the Lamp of Knowledge, Coordinator's Handbook and Volunteer's Handbook*, Logan Utah City Schools, n.d.; *A New Team: Business and the Schools*, Salt Lake City, Utah Schools, n.d., among the many sources reviewed.

8.

Future Trends

Community resources used in education are becoming increasingly important. Review of the current literature reflects growing interest in action learning, community-based learning, total-life simulation projects, and other concepts which utilize community resources. Teachers, administrators, and parents are awakening to the need to expand the use of volunteers, senior citizens, and various community agencies in the schools. The future will see more use of community resources at all levels of education.

Probabilities, Possibilities, and Practicalities

The educator of the future will face tremendous changes in concepts of education. Industry/education/community mergers of efforts to enhance learning are already before us with school efforts such as Philadelphia's Parkway Program. Some have proposed that the creation of an educational-industrial complex would change the nature of learning. In industrial/ business organizations, education (training) is viewed as an "overhead" cost, and efforts must be made to make it as efficient as possible in terms of time and learning. In current educational institutions, education is viewed as a "product," with less concern for the time taken for learners to achieve competencies. When teachers attempt to innovate to improve learning and decrease the time required for the process, they are usually discouraged. This will not likely be the trend of the future.

Authors outside education have been critical of the human waste of labor-intensive efforts associated with learning in the schools. On the contrary, in business and industrial settings, huge investments are made in planning and applications of technology (including machines, but also including the use of scientific and organized knowledge). Education has been absorbing more and more financial resources in labor. It takes more and more human effort in the schools. There is no way that education can continue this way because the money is simply not there! To get past the fiscal problem of being overly labor-intensive, we must find ways to legitimatize and more fully use community resources. We cannot afford, as educators or as members of society, to allow education to continue with "business as usual."

Formal education may become more community based to include libraries, museums, media centers, and community centers, which may also gain the right to issue degrees and certificates. Home learning centers are feasible with the development of videodisc/microcomputer systems to be supplied with mass produced and distributed materials, which are already less expensive than the traditional book. The economic realities will make the possibilities more practical.

Marshall McLuhan and others have pointed out the changing nature of information and education, stating that the child of the 19th century knew that it was necessary to attend school to gain access to the major sources of information and learning. It was an "information scarce" society in which the young learned largely through books and print media; or the interpretation of the same information by teachers provided the needed learning. Geographical horizons were as limited as the scope of vicarious learning resources. The child of the 20th century is becoming increasingly aware that his or her community and home environments are *more* "information rich" than the school! The child sees schooling, at times, as *detracting* from his or her real education.

It is now difficult to have an experience that is not interpreted by radio and television, several times, before it is discussed in the school room. The information curriculum of the past no longer remains viable, and firsthand experiences have increased in value for learning from the non-school environment of the community. Experiences of participation in theater or ballet, a concert, or the administration of a library or museum; of writing news; the development of photographic displays; assisting with social services to help those who cannot help themselves—all add to the learning of content and of important attitudes.

Summary

Community resources used in education will become much more important in the future. Trends are based upon the needs, goals, and practices of the entire community, from our homes, schools, businesses, professions, arts, trades, and communication media. The future points to greater use of community resources, based upon demographic, technological, social, cultural, ecological, and information factors as they interact to bring change in our society, communities, and schools. The probabilities, possibilities, and practicalities all point to the need for more "firsthand" experiences to be provided by more effective utilization of community resources in education.

9.

Suggested Student Project Activities

Several competencies, including surveying, identifying, describing, and cataloging community resources so as to provide for effective utilization in the teaching-learning process, were listed at the beginning of this book. It was suggested that the local telephone directory, blank cards, or printed forms for a looseleaf binder be used to set up a community resources file. This task was considered complete when it included sources for field trips, resource persons, instructional materials which might be identified from the community, and institutions useful for learning or instructional purposes. Suggested learning activities included the listing of procedures for conducting community surveys; the effective planning and conducting of field trips (sometimes called study trips); identifying several institutions and agencies which may be utilized as learning resources, such as planetariums, aquariums, banks, and industries; and the identification of resource persons in the community-at-large, including state, regional, or national locations. It is important that students "do" some of the activities suggested, rather than only read or listen to content descriptions. Students who do the activities will have greater retention of the learning and much greater understanding.

1. Selected learners will be given a specific curriculum guide or topic, along with a local telephone directory and blank cards or looseleaf binder forms. They will identify and

describe several community resources, including no fewer than two in each of the categories of (1) resource persons, (2) institutions and agencies, (3) businesses and industries, and (4) instructional materials which may be used in a unit of instruction. The listing should also classify the resources and suggest feasible guidelines for their use within the assigned curriculum topic.

2. Selected learners will go into the community, with a telephone directory, and write a document for setting up a curriculum utilizing only community resources. The curriculum will be limited to one field of learning, such as music, theater, business education, physical education, home economics, etc. The activity will be considered adequately completed when a dozen resources from the community are identified, described, and written into a feasible plan as judged by a panel of two other students and the instructor. It is suggested that the learners selected be placed in teams in order to better organize the management of this learning task. The completed written document will include in addition to the identified and described community resources (1) a rationale for their use, such as identified as "action learning" in this book; (2) procedures for the use of the resources; and (3) the anticipated outcomes of the planned learning.

3. Selected learners will identify resource persons who may be utilized in a series of three Telelectures for a curriculum area. They will obtain biographical data, telephone numbers and addresses, and draft short topical outlines to which the resource persons would direct their opening comments during a Telelecture lasting 30 minutes. After the three persons are identified, the outline is completed along with the questions, and arrangements are made to actually perform one live Telelecture with a resource person, using the plan as designated by the learners. The task is completed with a successful Telelecture.

4. In teams, selected learners will survey an assigned locale of the community and identify resources which may be utilized by individual learners or large groups. Such resources to be used may be museums, libraries, zoos, planetariums, businesses or industries, agencies, geographical or historical sites, or other such resources. The activity is considered successfully completed after a group of learners has utilized two resources and evaluated the learning as relevant and valuable to their learning.

5. Selected students will identify three possible sites for a field trip in a specified curriculum area, use the guidelines given in this book for field trips, and then plan a field trip. Following the planning, the students will conduct the field trip and provide a brief instrument for evaluation of the experience by the learners participating in the trip. The selected students conducting the field trip, under the supervision of the instructor, will follow all precautions and suggested procedures, including the transportation arrangements, the outline of the students' personal and financial responsibilities, and the written memorandum to the parents that is signed by the parents as deemed appropriate by the instructor. The activity is judged as successfully completed by a panel of three students, other than those planning the trip, and the instructor.

6. Selected students will survey a specified locale of a community as mutually approved by the students and the instructor, and one identified resource will be used as the basis for a report done by means other than writing, such as 8mm film, slide/audiotapes, videotape, or other media. It may include an art gallery, museum, shopping center, traffic survey, junked cars or other litter problem, or other areas which have been identified and mutually determined by the students and instructor to serve as a resource for learning. The activity is judged by a panel of three students and an instructor, other than the one for the course.

7. Selected students will identify a local resource person who has expertise in a hobby, profession, or occupation, and will conduct an interview of at least 15 minutes in duration. The students will prepare a skeleton outline of a topic, or describe a topic in no more than a paragraph for beginning the interview, and list three questions to which they would like the resource person to respond. The interview will be recorded on audiotape and played back to the class. The class will judge the task as either satisfactorily completed or inadequate. The students will continue with additional interviews until the majority judge the interview as satisfactorily completed. As an alternative, where equipment is available, videotape may be used.

8. Selected students will use a particular, specified school site, and survey the resources near the site, including parks, school grounds, visual resources, such as mountains, rivers, valleys, freeways, and buildings, and botanical resources, such as trees, bushes, and other plants. A site plan for incorporating existing resources into learning experiences will then be developed. The survey and plans will be judged adequate when three resources are identified or planned for three different areas of the curriculum and are rated by a panel consisting of an administrator, a teacher, and one student.

9. Selected students will identify a local geographical feature, such as a river, mountain, plain, cornfield, park, or other resource, and plan historical, musical, artistic, or written learning activities, using the selected geographical resource as the basis for input into the learning. The students will test the planned activity with a minimum of three learners from the group of learners for which the activity was planned. The activity will be judged as adequately completed when two of the three learners rate the experience as meaningful and interesting to their learning as specified by their instructor.

The foregoing suggested student project activities are given as examples of what might be done when actually involving students with the effective utilization of community resources in the teaching-learning process. Many others may be developed by creative instructors and students who have grasped the ideas and concepts presented in this book. Learning resources abound all around us and must only be identified, surveyed, described, and cataloged; then, learning activities must be specified and tested to make learning more relevant and meaningful. When these tasks are begun, the gap between learning and the real world is reduced, and the isolation of the schools from the community in which they are located is diminished.

The task of surveying, identifying, categorizing, describing, cataloging, and effectively utilizing community resources in the teaching-learning process is never completed. Just as the needs of the curriculum and learners change, so the community changes, and the possibilities of its use in education increase. Future trends indicate community resources will be used more and more in the teaching-learning process, and educators should become better able to plan and implement such activities. Although this sentence ends the body of this book, it is hoped that "from this ending springs new beginnings." The development of these new beginnings depends upon educators who utilize effectively community resources to enhance learning.

10.

Glossary

Action Learning

Often is called "community-based learning." A learning situation in which students learn not in a classroom, but rather by using the cultural, governmental, business and industrial, people, materials, events, institutional, service, and physical resources of the community as motivation and learning tools. The key component to action learning is that the student learns by actually participating, such as tutoring others and working with a community, organization, or industry.

Community Resource Council

An advisory board, including membership from parents, community service agencies, industry and business, students, and the school administration and faculty, which helps with the development of decision-making and policy concerning use of community resources. The board serves to initiate new changes and to communicate to the community the purpose of "community-based learning."

Community Resources

Resources of a community, which while not designed as learning resources, can be used by people to meet their learning needs and interests. Examples of community resources include museums, governmental agencies, parks and playgrounds, cultural events, businesses and industries, and social service agencies.

Community School

An elementary, secondary, and/or adult/continuing education organizational arrangement (or institution) operated by a local board of public education in which instruction and other activities are intended to be relevant and applicable to the needs of all or most segments of the total population of the community served.

Computer-Assisted Instruction (CAI)

An instructional technique based on the two-way interaction of the learner and a computer with the objectives of human learning and retention. This technique of using the computer allows for individual, individually paced, and individualized instruction, since the computer's behavior is dependent upon the responses of the student. The computer contains stored instructional programs or controls the presentation of stimuli to the student and accepts and evaluates the student responses, and based on that interaction, presents further stimuli calculated to shape the student responses in a desired manner. Such instruction may include problem-solving, drill and practice, inquiry, simulation and gaming, tutorial instruction, dialogue systems, and testing.

Continuous Progress Curricula

Means and techniques are provided to allow for continuous progression in difficulty from one stage of learning to the next.

Deployment

Placed in a new organization, or different uses, or simply the placement of media or funds in harmony with assessed needs and priorities set by the application of the systems approach to the use of the learning resources.

Free School

Instructional programs set up to be separate from the traditional school system and to be more relevant to learner needs by using experiences which are real rather than contrived for learning purposes. Action learning is related to the free school movement. The "free university" is also related to the "free school," and was set up as an instructional program by dissident students and/or faculty members near some university centers as protests against alleged irrelevant educational programs.

Media Learning

In the past, "book learning" has been the major mode for disseminating information associated with learning. The trend with the impact of TV and public educational programming, such as *The Electric Company* and *Sesame Street*, has been directed to "media learning" in the sense that people formerly spoke of "book learning."

Nongradedness

Related to learning in which groups of students and individuals are organized by academic ability, disciplinary problems, and mental or physical capabilities rather than by grade levels and age.

Open Education

A variety of groups or classes may be working at the same time at different grade levels on different subjects. Often the "open classroom" is utilized which is a relatively large instructional area or multiple-classroom space not separated by walls. The "open school" is the same type of idea, but applied to an entire school population and plant. Some have described the open school as one large media center, with flexible space which may be used for the particular learning activity needed by small groups, large groups, and individuals.

Pedagogy

The art, practice, and/or profession of teaching. It is the systematized learning or instruction concerning principles and methods of teaching and of student control and guidance.

Steering Committee

A committee utilized in school instructional development activities which is concerned with the organization and coordination of materials, facilities, and personnel to enhance learning.

Tutorial Group

Related to a process of learning originally used in colleges where the instructional staff work with groups of students assigned to them in individual conferences. Rather than as formalized classes with lectures and other group instructional methods being utilized, meetings are arranged as needed, allowing students more flexibility in their own learning styles and depth of learning. The tutorial plan, as developed at Harvard University, is designed to provide specific individual guidance in learning by assignment of students to individual instructors whose responsibility is to develop effective study habits in the student and relate his or her intellectual activities to his or her whole life. It is also used to designate the assignment of students to tutors who assist in solving special problems of scholarship and research relating to designated areas.

Visual Learning

Recently, special attention has focused on the lack of attention of educators to the visual world of their students and how they learn through visual images. This trend has caused one large oil company to actually invest millions of dollars into diversification of business to what they call "imagery." Visual literacy has been another manifestation of this activity, which is the ability to perceive the content of a message being communicated through visual means, other than print or writing. When perceptual skills are developed, they enable a visual, literate person to discriminate and interpret visual actions, objects, or symbols, natural or man-made, that he or she may encounter in the environment.

11.

Bibliography

"Action Education." Special issue of *National Association of Secondary School Principals Bulletin,* November, 1974.

"Action-Learning: Background and Development." *Education Digest,* March, 1975, pp. 2-5.

Allen, L.E. "Community Thinkers' Tournaments for Coordinating Other Community Resources to Complete the Educational Function of Schools." *Journal of Educational Technology Systems,* Volume VI, 1977-78, pp. 371-383.

Altman, S.M. *et al.* "Reality Classrooms: Field Experience and Undergraduate Education." *Improving College and University Teaching,* Winter, 1978, pp. 56-70.

Andres, H.A. *et al.* "Impacting Home Health Care Services: A Community-Based Approach." *Community College Frontiers,* Winter, 1978, pp. 6-10.

Armstrong, David G., and Savage, Tom V., Jr. "A Framework for Utilizing the Community for Social Learning in Grades 4 to 6." *Social Education,* March, 1976.

Bechtol, B. *et al.* "Creating a Regional Classroom; California Studies Program." *Phi Delta Kappan,* June, 1978, pp. 714-715.

Beder, H. "Practical Approach to Nonformal Adult Education." *Lifelong Learning: The Adult Years.* October, 1978, pp. 10-11.

Bell, L., and Connelly, D.M. "Get-Up-and-Go: Museum of Science, Boston." *Science and Children,* March, 1978, pp. 36-37.

Blackman, Nathaniel. "Metro: Experimental High School Without Walls." *National Association of Secondary School Principals Bulletin,* May, 1971.

Blair, M.J. "Utilizing Community Resources for Health Education Program of a Technical College." *Journal of the American College Health Association,* April, 1978, pp. 273-274.

Bobowski, Rita Cipalla. "College Model for the Grassroots." *American Education,* June, 1976, pp. 14-16.

Borhegyi, Stephan F., and Dodson, Elba A. *A Bibliography of Museums and Museum Work, 1900-1960,* in two volumes. Milwaukee Public Museum, 1961.

Bremer, John. "ABC's of City Learning." *Saturday Review,* August 19, 1972.

Brown, James W. *et al. AV Instruction: Technology, Media, and Methods.* Fourth Edition. New York: McGraw-Hill, 1973.

Brown, Sandra. *A. Guide. Life Situations: Incorporating Community Resources into the Adult ESL Curriculum.* March 5, 1978, p. 27.

Buggey, JoAnne. "Citizenship and Community Involvement." *Social Studies and the Elementary Teacher,* March, 1976, p. 161.

"Calendar of Class Field-Trip Ideas and Resources." *Forecast for Home Economics,* October, 1977, pp. 34-35.

Calhoun, Oliva H. *Teacher's Manual for the Career Development Curriculum Guides, 7th and 8th Grades.* Bureau of Adult, Vocational, and Technical Education, 1972, 70 pp.

California State Department of Education. *Career Education: A Position Paper on Career Development and Preparation in California.* Career Education Task Force, 1974, 27 pp.

Campbell, D., and Jensen, R. "Community and Family History at the Newberry Library: Some Solutions to a National Need." *History Teacher,* November, 1977, pp. 47-54.

Chalmers, John J. "Exploring Local Resources." *Audiovisual Instruction*, May, 1971.

Chedsey, K.A. "All About the Dentist." *Instructor,* 1977.

Clark, P.A. "Community Education and Its Major Components." *Journal of Teacher Education*, July-August, 1977, pp. 5-8.

Colorado State Facilitator Project, Longmount. *Resource Guide to Career Education in Colorado.* U.S. Office of Education, Washington, D.C., March, 1975, 74 pp.

Committee on Human Resources of the Metropolitan School Study Council. *Fifty Teachers to a Classroom.* New York: Macmillan, 1953.

Community Education Need/Resource Assessment: A Summary Report. Pennsbury, Pennsylvania, 1976.

Community Resource Guide. York County School District, Rock Hill, South Carolina, September, 1975, 435 pp.

Conk, J.A.S. "Using Community Language Resources in the Schools." *Theory into Practice,* December, 1977, pp. 401-406.

Cook, S.A. "Delphi Connection or Public Library Know Thyself." *Wilson Library Bulletin,* May, 1978, pp. 703-706.

Cooley, A.P. "Community-Issues Biology: A Different Kind of Action-Learning." *American Biology Teacher,* November, 1976, pp. 469-472.

Cross, David. "The Pedagogy of Participation." *Teachers College Record,* December, 1974, pp. 316-334.

Croteau, S. "You Call Us: They'll Call You: Learning Exchange." *Education Digest,* April, 1977, pp. 16-18.

Cruz, Rodolfo, and Segura, Roberto. *The Potential Application of the Model Learning Concept to a Chicano Studies Curricula in the Community College.* National Center for Educational Research and Development, Washington, D.C., August, 1973, 31 pp.

Curtis, Anthony R. "Where Students Pay Back Their Community." *American Education,* April, 1976, pp. 26-30.

Danilov, V.J. "Museums Are Coming Alive: Innovative Approaches of Science Centers." *American Biology Teacher,* December, 1976, pp. 524-527.

Davies, Ruth Ann. *The School Library Media Center: A Force for Educational Excellence.* Second Edition. New York: R.R. Bowker, 1974.

Decker, Larry E. *People Helping People: An Overview of Community Education.* Midland, Michigan: Pendell Publishing Company, 1976.

Dennison, D. "Effects of Selected Field Experiences upon the Drinking Behavior of University Students." *Journal of School Health,* January, 1977, pp. 38-41.

Department of Rural Education, NEA. *Community Resources in Rural Schools.* Washington, D.C.: National Education Association, 1959.

Deutschlander, Gary H. "Action-Learning: The Curriculum Beyond the School." *Education Digest,* February, 1975, pp. 60-63.

Drews, Pearl A. *Flight Plan: Toward a Career Choice. School and Community as Co-Pilots of Career Education.* Akron Public Schools, 1977, 405 pp.

Drumheller, Sidney J. *Handbook of Curriculum Design for Individualized Instruction: A Systems Approach.* Englewood Cliffs, New Jersey: Educational Technology Publications, 1971.

Duane, James E. *et al. Individualized Instruction—Programs and Materials.* Englewood Cliffs, New Jersey: Educational Technology Publications, 1972.

Duet, C., and Newfield, J. "Labor: An Untapped Resource in Career Education." *National Association of Secondary School Principals Bulletin,* April, 1978, pp. 50-59.

Edling, Jack V. *Individualized Instruction: A Manual for Administrators.* Corvallis, Oregon: Teaching Research Division of the Oregon State System of Higher Education, 1972.

Eldredge, C.C. "Museum as Educator: The Helen Foresman Spencer Museum of Art." *Art Journal,* Spring, 1978, pp. 245-247.

Ethnic Resource Guide: An Annotated Bibliography for Teachers. Illinois State Office of Education, Chicago, August, 1975, 64 pp.

Fagan, E.R. "Community-Based Resources for Teaching Composition." *English Journal,* November, 1976, pp. 61-64.

Falkenstein, L.C. "Action Learning: A Model for In-Service Teacher Education." *The Clearing House,* January, 1977, pp. 188-191.

Fawcett, S.B., and Fletcher, R.K. "Community Application of Instructional Technology: Training Writers of Instructional Packages." *Journal of Applied Behavioral Analysis,* Winter, 1977, pp. 739-746.

Fein, Albert, and Gatner, Elliot (Eds.). *University and Community: The New Partnership.* Brooklyn, New York: Long Island University, 1971.

Finn, P. "Making the Most of Community Resources." *Music Educators Journal,* March, 1977, pp. 44-48.

Fischer, John H. "Who Needs Schools?" *Saturday Review,* September 19, 1970.

Fleming, L.D. "Community Education and Public Libraries: Cooperation or Conquest?" *Wilson Library Bulletin,* December, 1977, pp. 319-323.

Frates, Mary Y. "Oklahoma City: A Working Partnership in the Arts." *National Elementary School Principals Bulletin,* January, 1976.

Freeman, Patricia. *Pathfinder: An Operational Guide for the School Librarian.* New York: Harper and Row, 1975.

Gibbons, Maurice. "What Is Individualized Instruction?" *Interchange,* 1970, pp. 28-52.

Gillespie, John T., and Spirit, Diana L. *Creating a School Media Program.* New York: R.R. Bowker, 1973.

Gjelten, Tom. *Schooling in Isolated Communities.* Maine State Department of Educational and Cultural Services, August, 1978, 106 pp.

Goldstein, R. "Art Insights: Making Senses." *Art Teacher,* Spring, 1978, pp. 22-23.

Gonino, V.J., and Haley, N. "Cortland's Historic Houseboat: An Outdoor Education Museum." *Journal of Physical Education and Recreation,* September, 1976, p. 52.

Good, Carter V. (Ed.) *Dictionary of Education.* Second Edition. New York: McGraw-Hill, 1959.

Gragg, Betty A. "Our Mighty Mississippi." *School Arts,* June, 1976.

Greenberg, A. "City-as-School: An Approach to External Interdisciplinary Education." *English Journal,* October, 1976, pp. 60-62.

Hager, Donna L. *et al. Community Involvement for Classroom Teachers.* Community Collaborators, Charlottesville, Virginia, July, 1977, 63 pp.

Hamilton, Arlene A., and Girard, Gayle S. "The Community as a Classroom." *Journal of Home Economics,* March, 1976, pp. 7-10.

Hammerman, Donald R., and Hammerman, William M., compilers. *Outdoor Education: A Book of Readings.* Minneapolis, Minn., 1968, 401 pp.

Hands-on Museums: Partners in Learning: A Report from Educational Facilities Laboratories, 1975, 44 pp.

Hansen, Roberta Jane M. "Self-Instruction Workbook and Slide/Tape Program: A Community Resource File for the Media Center." Unpublished Practicum Report, Utah State University, 1975.

Harlacher, E.L., and Gollattscheck, J.R. "Implementing Community-Based Education; Symposium." *New Directions for Community Colleges,* Spring, 1978, pp. 1-102.

Haslam, L. "Community Director in Massachusetts." *Instructor,* January, 1978, p. 59.

Hechinger, F.M. "Schools Without Schools." *Education Digest,* October, 1977, pp. 10-13.

Henriksen, Dorothy (Ed.). *A Model for a School-Community Resource Directory.* Roseville Area School District 623, Minn., 1978, 21 pp.

Hickey, Howard W. "Community Education's Implications for Teachers." *Journal of Teacher Education,* July-August, 1977, pp. 19-20.

Hiemstra, Roger. *The Community Perspective for Research on Lifelong Learning.* March 28, 1978, 21 pp.

Hitchens, Howard, Wallington, James C., and Hawkins, Susan D. *Educational Technology: A Handbook of Standard Terminology and a Guide for Recording and Reporting Information About Educational Technology.* Washington, D.C.: U.S. Government Printing Office, 1975.

Hodges, Patrick B. "Unlimited Facilities on a Limited Budget." *Journal of Physical Education and Recreation,* April, 1976, p. 25.

Hofman, H. "Resource People." *Science and Children,* Fall, 1978, pp. 20-21.

Houston, Robert W. *et al. Resources for Performance-Based Education.* Albany, New York: University of the State of New York, 1973.

Howard, Eugene R. "Individualized Instruction." *Encyclopedia of Education,* edited by Lee C. Deighton. New York: Macmillan, 1971.

Hoyt, Kenneth. *Community Resources for Career Education.* Washington, D.C.: U.S. Government Printing Office, 1976.

Hunter, Made Line. "Tailor Your Teaching to Individualized Instruction." *Instructor,* March, 1970, pp. 53-54.

Hurt, R.D. "Agricultural Museums: A New Frontier for the Social Sciences." *History Teacher,* May, 1978, pp. 367-375.

"Idea Bank: Using Community Resources." *Music Educators Journal,* January, 1977, pp. 50-54.

Irwin, Martha, and Russell, Wilma. *The Community Is the Classroom.* Midland, Michigan: Pendell Publishing Company, 1971.

Journal of Teacher Education, Special Community Education Issue, July-August, 1977.

Karant, V.I. "Socrates Denied: A Defeat for Community Resource People in the Public Schools." *Phi Delta Kappan,* April, 1977, pp. 639-641.

Keats, E.J. "Discovering the Library." *Teacher,* December, 1976, pp. 40-41.

Kepner, Tom, and Sparks, Lanny. *What You Always Wanted to Know About Performance Objectives but Were Afraid to Ask.* Syracuse, New York: National Special Media Institutes, 1972.

Kindred, Lucian L. *More Than Magic: Community Resources for Career Education. A Practical Guidebook.* Industry-Education Council of Burlingame, California, 1977.

Knoblock, Peter *et al. Preparing Humanistic Teachers for Troubled Children.* Syracuse University Division of Special Education and Rehabilitation, January, 1974, 142 pp.

Marsh, Colin J. "Whatever Happened to Local Community Studies?" *The Clearing House,* February, 1976.

Mathews, R.M., and Fawcett, S.B. "Community Applications of Instructional Technology: Training Low-Income Proctors." *Journal of Applied Behavioral Analysis,* Winter, 1977, pp. 747-754.

May, Jim. "Community Culture—A Course with Class." *English Journal,* March, 1976.

McClure, Larry *et al. Experience-Based Learning: How to Make the Community Your Classroom.* Northwest Regional Educational Laboratory, Portland, Oregon, July, 1977.

McDanield, Michael A. "Tomorrow's Curriculum Today." In *Learning for Tomorrow: The Role of the Future in Education,* edited by Alvin Toffler. New York: Random House, 1974.

Metcalf, Fay D., and Downey, Matthew T. *Teaching Local History: Trends, Tips, and Resources.* Sponsored by the National Institute of Education, Boulder Colorado Science Education Consortium, Inc., 1977, 110 pp.

Minneapolis Public Schools. *Marcy Open School Community Day Program Report.* Sponsored by the National Institute of Education, June, 1974, 30 pp.

Mirsly, M. "Ivory Towers and City Walls." *Chronicle of Higher Education,* June 18, 1977, p. 32.

Moore, F.R., and Ratchner, C.A. "Spanish? Mexican? Chicano? The Influence of Spanish Culture on New Mexico; Community Survey." *Integrated Education,* September, 1976, pp. 23-24.

Museums, Imagination, and Education. UNESCO, Paris, 1973, 148 pp.

Museums: Their New Audience. A Report to the Department of Housing and Urban Development by a Special Committee of the American Association of Museums, July, 1972, 112 pp.

Newmann, Fred M. *Education for Citizen Action.* Berkeley, California: McCutchan, 1975.

Newsom, B.Y. "Art Museum and the School." *American Education,* December, 1977, pp. 12-16.

Nicol, Marjorie, and Jordan, Gail. *The Community Is Our Classroom.* TEAL Occasional Papers, Vol. I, 1977. British Columbia Association of Teachers of English as an Additional Language, Vancouver, B.C., 1977.

Norfuls, D. "Community Resources for Economics Education." *Social Studies,* November-December, 1977, pp. 58-61.

Nyberg, David (Ed.). *The Philosophy of Open Education.* Boston, Mass.: Routledge and Kegan Paul, 1975.

"The Opportunity to Test Theory with Reality: Action-Learning-Background and Development." *Education Digest,* March, 1975, p. 2.

Parson, Steve R. *Emerging Models of Community Education.* Midland, Michigan: Pendell Publishing Company, 1976.

Paulsen, F. Robert (Ed.). *The University and Community Services: A Conference Sponsored by the Community Resources Project.* Tucson, Arizona: University of Arizona, 1969.

Penland, Patrick R., and Williams, James G. Community Psychology and Coordination. Vol. 4 in *Communication Science and Technology Series.* New York: Marcel Dekker, 1975.

Peters, Richard. *A Perspective of Career Education Program Development in Rural Schools.* June, 1978, 23 pp.

Peters, Richard O. *Discourse on the Anatomical Perspective of the World of Career Education: The Process of Occupational Awareness and Decision Making.* February, 1978, 42 pp.

Pokorny, T. "Art Day." *School Arts,* June, 1978, pp. 40-41.

Polette, Nancy. *Developing Methods of Inquiry: A Source Book for Elementary Media Personnel.* Metuchen, New Jersey: Scarecrow, 1973.

Price, J.H. "Field Trips." *Health Education,* May-June, 1978, p. 43.

Radford, Wendell C. "A Survey of Community Resources Available to the Midway Area Schools of School District 251, Jefferson County, Idaho." Unpublished Field Project, Brigham Young University, 1964.

Reed, M. "Community of Teachers." *English Education,* Winter, 1978, pp. 95-101.

Resnik, Henry S. "High School with No Walls." *The Education Digest,* March, 1970.

Ripley, S.D. "Education's Dilemma Today." *National Association of Secondary School Principals Bulletin,* December, 1977, pp. 84-88.

Ristau, Roberta. *Career Education in Secondary and Higher Education.* Eastern Michigan University, n.d., 10 pp.

Robinson, J. "Busing That Everyone Likes." *Library Journal,* January 15, 1978, pp. 142-143.

Rogers, V. "Crank Up Your Curriculum; Photo Essay." *Instructor,* August, 1976, pp. 62-63.

Sanders, P. "Grammar: The Tool of the Trades." *School and Community,* March, 1978, p. 14.

Santinelli, P. "Study Service That Can Benefit Both the Student and Society." *Times Higher Education Supplement,* August 18, 1978, p. 8.

Saunders, D. "Window Watchers; When Attention Goes Out the Window." *Learning,* April, 1978, p. 28.

"Scattered Sites Disperse 1,000 Pupils; SAND Everywhere School, Hartford." *American School and University,* August, 1977, pp. 32-33.

Schofield, Dee. *Community Schools.* Arlington, Virginia: National Association of Elementary School Principals, 1974.

Schrand, H.L., and Musa, K.E. "Museum as a Teaching Tool." *Journal of Home Economics,* March, 1978, pp. 28-31.

Schuller, Charles F. "Instructional Development Program of the University Consortium for Instructional Development and Technology." *Educational Media Yearbook,* 1973.

Serres, D.L. "Black Gold and Wildcats: Interviewing Local Residents." *Communication Education,* September, 1976, pp. 255-258.

Seskin, J. "Project: Adventure in a City Neighborhood." *Instructor,* May, 1978, p. 55.

Shane, Harold G., and Shane, June Grant. "Educating the Youngest for Tomorrow." *Learning for Tomorrow: The Role of the Future in Education,* edited by Alvin Toffler. New York: Random House, 1974.

Shaw, R., and Allan, Valois (Eds.). *Manual on Independent Learning Centers.* Kansas State University, Manhattan, 1974, 83 pp.

Shukyn, Murray. "Shared Experience, Exploration, and Discovery." *National Association of Secondary School Principals Bulletin,* May, 1971.

Shuttleworth, D. "Whatever Happened to Community Involvement?" *Education Canada,* Summer, 1977, pp. 26-29.

Silberman, A. "Snakeful of Learning." *Instructor,* February, 1978, p. 36.

Silver, A.Z. "Make a Museum Your Second Classroom." *Instructor,* October, 1978, pp. 96-98.

Sleeper, M.E. "Teaching About Work in History; A Museum Curriculum for the Schools." *History Teacher,* February, 1978, pp. 159-174.

Smellie, Don C. *Guidelines for Graduate Students in Instructional Media.* Logan, Utah: Department of Instructional Media, 1976.

Smith, E.T., and Winnick, P. "Your Library: Neighborhood Ombudsman; Neighborhood Information Center Helps Everyone." *American Education,* November, 1976, pp. 6-11.

Smith, Edward W., Krouse, Stanley W., and Atkinson, Mark M. *The Educator's Encyclopedia.* Englewood Cliffs, New Jersey: Prentice-Hall, 1961.

Somerville, T. "ACES, A Community Education Program." *National Association of Secondary School Principals Bulletin,* April, 1977, pp. 116-118.

Sparks, Lanny. *Prototype Specifications Manual.* Syracuse, New York: National Special Media Institutes, 1972.

Spector, P. "Help Around the Corner; Environmental Education Resource People." *Instructor,* October, 1976, p. 182.

Stillman, Susan, and Jordan, Barbra. "Open Schools and Citizenship-Education Through Involvement in the Community." *Social Education,* March, 1976.

Stocker, J. "Classroom in the Cactus: Arizona-Sonora Desert Museum." *American Education,* December, 1977, pp. 6-11.

Stranix, E., and Fleishman, M. "City Streets: Outdoor Classrooms." *Teacher,* October, 1977, pp. 87-88.

Sykes, Vivian, and Tricanao, Terese. *Reach: A Multicultural Education Resource Handbook for the San Francisco Bay Area.* Sponsored by the U.S. Office of Education, Stanford University School of Education, June, 1977, 51 pp.

Tait, S.F. "Community Analysis." *School Library Journal,* February, 1978, p. 42.

Taylor, C. *et al.* "Using Local Architecture as an Historical Resource: Some Teaching Strategies." *History Teacher,* February, 1978, pp. 175-192.

Taylor, D.T. "Community-Based Approach to Law-Related Education: The Cincinnati Model." *Peabody Journal of Education,* October, 1977, pp. 24-27.

"Technology, Libraries, and Public Relations: A Symposium." *Audiovisual Instruction,* February, 1977, pp. 9-26.

"These Kids Perform Community Services!" *Instructor,* January, 1978, pp. 60+.

Thomas, J. Alan. *Resource Allocation in Classrooms. Final Report.* Sponsored by the National Institute of Education, October 12, 1977, 128 pp.

Toffler, Alvin. "The Psychology of the Future." In *Learning for Tomorrow: The Role of the Future in Education,* edited by Alvin Toffler. New York: Random House, 1974.

Totten, W. Fred, and Manley, Frank J. *The Community School: Basic Concepts, Functions, and Organization.* Galien, Michigan: Allied Education Council, 1969.

Tregaskis, Lyle R. *A Guide for Elementary Teachers in Environmental Education.* American Fork, Utah: Alpine School District, 1970.

Trutko, H.M. "Community Agencies: Another Resource for Reaching Students." *Journal of the National Association of College Admissions Counselors,* September, 1977, pp. 20-21.

Unger, R.A. "Taking the Drug Problem to the Community." *American Secondary Education,* June, 1977, pp. 8-10.

Vandervoort, F.S. "City Parks: More Than Meets the Eye." *American Biology Teacher,* November, 1977, pp. 473-475.

Vermilye, Dyckman W. *Individualizing the System: Current Issues in Higher Education, 1976.* San Francisco: Jossey-Bass, 1976.

Wallat, C., and Goldman, R. "School Without Schools: How Columbus Met the Winter Energy Crisis." *Phi Delta Kappan,* April, 1977, pp. 642-643.

Wallesz, D.P. "Museum Approach to Environmental Education; Hall of Natural Science and Ecology at the Pennsylvania State Museum." *American Biology Teacher,* December, 1976, pp. 497-498.

Weisgerber, Robert A. "Individualized Instruction, Individualized Learning, and Independent Study." In *Educational Media Yearbook,* edited by James W. Brown. New York: R.R. Bowker, 1973.

Welsh, Mary McAnaw. "A Campus Goes to the Community." *Journal of Home Economics,* March, 1976.

Winecoff, Larry, and Powell, Conrad. *Focus: Seven Steps to Community Involvement in Education Problem-Solving.* Midland, Michigan: Pendell Publishing Company, 1975.

Wiper, H. "New Place for Final Examination: Science Museum." *American Biology Teacher,* May, 1978, p. 322.

Wittich, Walter Arno, and Schuller, Charles Francis. *Audiovisual Materials: Their Nature and Use.* Fourth Edition. New York: Harper and Row, 1967.

Wood, Rulon Kent. *Using Media Centers in Education: The NATUL Project.* Logan, Utah: Instructional Media Department of Utah State University, 1976.

Workman, B. "Into the Community with a Slide/Sound Show." *Media and Methods,* April, 1978, pp. 73-74.

Wright, Donald L., and Taylor, Teresa E. *School-Community Linking Agencies: A National Guide.* BICEP, Salt Lake City, 1978, 217 pp. (BICEP is an acronym for Business, Industry, Community, Education Partnership.)

Wurman, Richard Saul (Ed.). *Yellow Pages of Learning Resources.* Cambridge, Massachusetts: MIT Press, 1972.

Wysocki, J.L. "How to Teach Housing." *Journal of Home Economics,* May, 1977, pp. 13-17.

Zimmerman, R., Jr. "Community Resources Aid in Expansion of Curriculum." *National Association of Secondary School Principals Bulletin,* May, 1978, pp. 146-148.

Zopf, D., and Simon, A. "Wage Earning Artist." *Art Teacher,* Winter, 1978, p. 28.

12.

Media on Community Resources

Career Education, 16mm film, 24 min., color, sound, Informational Materials, Burbank, California, 1972. Stresses the integration of academic and vocational education, with the point that "preparation for work is preparation for life." It shows the effect of education on the world of work and society. Junior high school through adult.

Career Exploration: Building Trades—Construction; Business Equipment Repair; Data Processing—Computer Technology; Electronics—Communication and Media; Food Services; Graphic Services; Metalworking/Manufacturing; Personal Services—Servicing People; Plastics—Forming and Design; Printing—Communications and Media; Public Services—Public Utilities; Sales—Marketing; Trucking—Land Transportation. Presents overview of the various trades and careers listed above. May prove useful as an introduction to using community resource persons from the various careers and trade areas. The series has 55 frames for each area and may be adapted for use with primary through high school. Acoustifone Corp., 1973; 7428 Bellaire Ave., North Hollywood, California 91605.

Community Action Motion Pictures, nine 16mm films, range from 13-30 min., sound, color, Centron Educational Films, Lawrence, Kansas, 1970. A series of films dealing with different aspects of the community. High school through adult.

Community Action for Recreation, 16mm film, 27 min.,

sound, color, Montgomery Ward and Company, 1966. The use of existing community resources to better meet the leisure-time activities of citizens, such as greater use of the schools by the adult population. Junior high school through adult.

Community Council, multimedia kit, including a 22 min. film, color, sound; a 10 min. filmstrip with cassette; and workbook materials. The functions of a community council are stressed, providing a number of examples of types of community advisory groups. College and general. Informational Materials, Inc., 1976; Burbank, California.

Community Education, The Search, 16mm film, 28 min., color, sound, CBS, 1955. A report on an excellent example of integration of community resources used effectively in education, including the Louisville public library, the university, and the board of education in cooperation to make a learning campus of the entire community. Junior high school through adult.

Community Education Program, 16mm film, 27 min., black and white, McGraw-Hill, 1955. Depicts the Louisville public library, the university, and the board of education as making the community serve the needs of all learners. High school through adult.

Community Resources and Supportive Services, 16mm film, 30 min., sound, color, Maryland State Department of Education, Division of ITV, 1975. Shows that adult basic education is life-centered and uses an ABE instructor as the vehicle to explore the many community services available to meet the immediate needs of learners. College and general.

Community Resources in Teaching, 16mm film, 19 min., sound, black and white, University of Iowa, Iowa City, 1950. Although an older film, it remains the definitive motion picture treatment of effective utilization of community resources in education. College and adult.

Community Resources Workshop for Teachers, color, mixed with black and white filmstrip, 59 frames, American Iron and Steel Institute, 1000 16th Street, NW, Washington, D.C., 1956. Although rather dated, this filmstrip remains useful in explaining an approach to plan and operate a community resources workshop where teachers can learn to utilize their communities as laboratories for improved teaching and learning.

Educational Field Trips for Young Children, slide-tape (cassette and script with 40 2" x 2"), color, Childhood Resources, Inc., Arlington, Virginia, 1971. Describes the experience of a field trip for children in nursery school, Kindergarten, and the primary grades. Primary grades.

Field Trip, filmstrip with captions, black and white, 36 frames, Simmel Meservey, Inc., n.d. Outlines steps in planning a successful field trip.

Field Trip, filmstrip, color, with captions, 35 frames, McGraw-Hill Films, 1970. Explains how to plan a field trip and outlines the rules to be followed while on the trip. (From *The School—Rules and Plans Series.*)

Field Trip Enrichment—A Series, including: More About the State Capitol, 89 frames; The Other Side of the Zoo, 91 frames; When You Visit an Industry, 81 frames; Who Are "They" at the Art Gallery?, 77 frames; Centron Educational Films, 1974. Primary and intermediate grades. Explores various career classifications and functions not normally seen or understood by students in their day-to-day contact with the community, region, or state.

Field Trip to the Seashore, filmstrip with sound on 33 1/3 rpm record, Bailey Films, 1971. (From the series and kit: *Science of the Sea,* distributed by BFA Educational Media, 2211 Michigan Avenue, P.O. Box 1795, Santa Monica, CA 90406.)

Field Trip—A Career Exploration Program—A Series, filmstrips with record or cassette and script, color, Macmillan

Films, Inc., 1976. Examines the transportation, service, entertainment, and fashion industries. Includes: Entertainment—Music Recording Industry; Fashion—Clothing Manufacturer; Service—Hotel Industry; Transportation—Airline Industry.

Field Trips for Discovery, 16mm film, 18 min., color, sound, McGraw-Hill, 1964. Explains the various types of field trips useful in science instruction and relates to making the "direct learning" experiences meaningful. High school and college level.

Field Trips for Fun and Facts—A Series, color filmstrips with sound tape, Prentice-Hall Media, 1970. Offers suggestions on how to get the most information and enjoyment from the exhibits in museums and zoos. Describes the skills and talents of those who run these centers, pointing out career opportunities in these fields. Series includes: Enjoying Art at a Museum; Experiencing History at a Museum; Investigating Science at a Museum; Meeting the Animals at a Zoo; What Is a Museum?

Field Trips Out of the Ordinary—A Series, filmstrips with audiotape, color, Eye Gate House, Inc., 1972. Describes the basic processes and elements of various industries and fields, including: Coal Mine, 51 frames; Lumber Mill, 42 frames; Nuclear Plant, 38 frames; Oil Well, 52 frames; Science for the Future, 53 frames; Steel Mill, 44 frames.

Field Trips Without Travel—A Series, filmstrips with records or cassettes and script, color, Teaching Resources Films, 1975. Shows behind-the-scenes of four modern institutions in order to teach children about a variety of places of employment. The series includes: The Airport, 62 frames; The Hospital, 62 frames; The Newspaper Office, 62 frames; The Television Studio, 62 frames.

Inside Out: Saving Our Urban Schools, 16mm film, 56 min., sound, color, Jack Roberston, 1970. Demonstrates the use of community business, industry, along with cultural resources and services to provide high school students with learning as exemplified by the Philadelphia Franklin Parkway Program. Secondary through adult levels.

Learning for Life, 16mm film, 28 min., color, sound. Provides background and an overview of how adult education programs relate to communities and public education. National Education Association, 1962. Adult.

Library World, 16mm film, 16 min., sound, color, Informational Materials, Inc., Burbank, California, 1977. A young boy is convinced libraries are a "drag" until the young librarian drives into his life to show how books helped him keep his sports car in shape. Intermediate.

Museum Is a Place to Learn—A Series, filmstrips with records or cassettes and script, color, Urban Media Materials, 1977. Introduces students to the world of museums and to the learning opportunity museum visits can provide. The series includes an Introduction; Learning About Art in Museums; Learning Geography in Museums; Learning History in Museums; Learning Science in Museums; Small Museums and Restorations. Primary through junior high levels.

Museum Serves the Community, filmstrip with captions, black and white, Visual Education Consultants, n.d. Although now out of print, this filmstrip is available in many library media centers, and remains useful. It discusses the fact that museums have become an important factor in the educational program of their own communities. Shows how exhibits and services display an understanding of the arts of man, the antiquities of history, and the wonders of nature. It stimulates interest in visiting museums and may be used with intermediate to adult audiences.

Museums and Man—A Series, filmstrips with records or cassettes and scripts, color, Encyclopaedia Britannica Educational Corp., 1975. The filmstrips include: An Exhibit—Behind the Scenes (Smithsonian Institution), 87 frames; Museum Conservation—Preserving Our Heritage, 89 frames; Museums—New Directions, 84 frames; What Is a Museum?, 93 frames; and The Zoo—A Living Collection, 87 frames. The series is useful with intermediate through college-age level in presenting the many varied aspects of museums of all types.

Museums: To Use and Enjoy, 16mm film, 12 min., sound, color, Coronet, 1977. Shows a group of youngsters on a tour of a museum where they learn to learn from the exhibits which are related to their school work. The film was produced in cooperation with the Field Museum of Natural History located in Chicago.

Open School, 16mm film, sound, color, Harper and Row, 1973.

A Park Community, 16mm film, 10 min., color, sound, Barr Films, 1974. Depicts how all living things depend upon their environment for survival, and in turn contribute to their community in which they live; done with especially interesting photography techniques. Primary through junior high school.

The Field Trip, 2-inch videotape, 30 min., black and white, Great Plains Instructional TV Library, University of Nebraska, P.O. Box 80669, Lincoln, Nebraska, n.d. Explains to the science teacher that field trips are an integral part of the total science program and should provide children with a reasonable amount of freedom to explore the environment as their interests direct them. (From *The Science Classroom Series* produced by WENH-TV, University of New Hampshire.)

The Learning Society, 16mm film, 20 min., color, sound, American Association for Higher Education, 1973. Depicts the sharing of traditional higher education functions with other agencies, including servicemens' opportunity college, labor study center, and the University Without Walls, through non-traditional study. The film relates practical life experiences and knowledge to academic credit. College and general.

The Librarian, 16mm, 10 min., sound, color, BFA Educational Media, 1970. Children learn through the film about the resources of a community library, including these human resources along with others, showing the resources other than books. Primary through intermediate grades.

The Park, 16mm film, 7 min., sound, color, Communico, Inc., Fenton, Missouri, 1970. Narration is minimal, made up of lines from Thoreau's *Walden,* and contrasts the urban, hurried atmosphere with the tranquility of the island of nature existent in the city park. Intermediate through adult.

Using Community Resources, slide-tape (cassette and script with 71 2" x 2"), color, University of Wisconsin Extension Services, 1970. Explains the process of planning to use community resources in youth programs and how needs may be identified and resources secured and sustained. (From *The Passport to Leadership Series,* which also includes: Arranging for Learning; Designing Learning Experiences; Growth and Development of Youth; Purpose of Youth Programs; Values; and Working with Youth, all of which may be useful to develop "using community resources" programs.) Adult level. Also available as a sound 35mm filmstrip.

What Is a Community? 16mm film, 16 min., color, sound, Encyclopaedia Britannica Education Corp., 1970. The film contrasts life in a rural setting with urban life, pointing out the different occupations found in each, and the problems associated with each type of community and the needs. The film is helpful for review prior to utilizing various community businesses and industrial resources for education, if the audience is prepared as to how they should view the motion picture. Primary and intermediate grades.

Your Community Is a Classroom, 16mm film, 28 min.,

sound, color, American Iron and Steel Institute, New York, or Capital Film Services, Lansing, Michigan, 1968. Elementary through adult learners may benefit from this film in seeing the relationship of using community resources in education.

Zoo, 16mm film, 21 min., color, sound, Doubleday Multimedia, 1974. A documentary on the National Zoo in Washington, D.C., which portrays the staff roles and the view of the Zoo through public eyes. Primary through junior high school.

Zoo, 16mm film, 12 min., black and white, sound, Pyramid Film, 1975. A characterization in humor with views of both sides of the bars, which portray the fundamental relationship of all living creatures. Junior high school through adult.

About the Author

Rulon Kent Wood holds graduate degrees from Denver, Western Michigan, and Brigham Young Universities with studies in Information, Instructional, and Library Sciences. His doctorate at BYU was in Higher Education Administration, with the other areas combined as areas of emphasis. He pioneered with research and development in videodisc/microcomputer technologies at Utah State University, where he directs the Videodisc Innovation Project.

Dr. Wood has special interests in systems analysis and management as well as instructional development and evaluation. He has directed more than 30 Instructional Development Institutes for the University Consortium for Instructional Development and Technology and is currently chairperson of the Association for Educational Communications and Technology's Definition and Terminology Committee. He has experience in school, public, university, and special library/media programs, and considers effective utilization of community resources by educators at all levels to be major means of improving the quality of life and learning.